CHESTER CATHEDRAL

FOREWORD

Chester Cathedral is many things to many people: a living community of worship, an ancient abbey, a cultural hub, a centre of musical excellence, a place of prayer and pilgrimage and a unique blend of modern and medieval history.

Christians have gathered to worship on this site for over a thousand years. We hope that your visit today will inspire you, and help you to connect the things of the earth with the wonder of heaven.

From the time of its foundation by monks who followed the rule of St Benedict, this has been a special place. Here at Chester Cathedral we are committed to living out the Benedictine tradition of welcome and hospitality in all that we do, and we very much hope that you enjoy your time exploring our magnificent building.

The Very Reverend Professor Gordon McPhate
Dean of Chester

ABOVE Musical angels in the windows on the north side of the nave.

OPPOSITE The tranquil cloister garden at the heart of monastic Chester.

CONTENTS

OPPOSITE This angel roundel is a detail from the Easton window in the north quire aisle.

CATHEDRAL TIMELINE

75
Deva (Chester) founded by Romans

313
Christianity legalized in Roman Empire

380
Christianity becomes the official Roman religion; a church may have been built at Chester

660
Saxon church founded by King Wulfhere, dedicated to Sts Peter and Paul

875
Queen Ethelflaeda brings St Werburgh's relics to Chester; church rededicated in Werburgh's honour

1092
Benedictine monastery founded by Hugh Lupus, earl of Chester. Building begins in the Romanesque (Norman) style

c.1220
Romanesque church finished

1225–30
Chapter house built in new Gothic style

c.1270
Lady Chapel built in new style

1280–90
Quire rebuilt in new style

1300
Crossing rebuilt

1350
South transept rebuilt

1360
South side of nave rebuilt

1490
North side of nave rebuilt; south transept closed off as parish church

1515
West front built, upper nave windows constructed

1540
Monastery dissolved, 4 February; building ceases, leaving church unfinished

1537–39
Vaulted stone ceiling in cloisters

KING·HENRY·VIII·ESTABLISHING·THE·SEE·OF·CHESTER·

1541
Henry VIII signs
letters patent creating
cathedral, 4 July;
church made as
useable as possible

1868–76
Large-scale
restoration under
George Gilbert Scott

1921–26
Stained glass installed
in cloisters

2016
South transept as
art gallery

1660s
St Anselm's chapel
adapted and enlarged
for bishop

1939
New refectory ceiling

1830s
Restoration work
begins

1900–02
South transept
ceiling built

1961
West window installed

1975
Separate Bell Tower
opened

1636
Consistory court
moved from Lady
Chapel to unfinished
south-west tower

1880
South transept
becomes part of
cathedral again
after 400 years

2013
Falconry opened in
Dean's Field

1911–13
East, north and west
cloister restored by
Giles Gilbert Scott

2003
Song School
completed

1835
Stained glass
re-introduced

1997
New stone floor and
under-floor heating
in nave

1992
Westminster
Windows in nave

Introduction

CHESTER CATHEDRAL ONLY BECAME A CATHEDRAL, THE SEAT OF A BISHOP, in 1541, as a result of Henry VIII's establishment of the Anglican church and his dissolution of the monasteries. For hundreds of years before that, the present building was a monastic church. Benedictine monks lived and worshipped here from the 1190s onwards, dedicating their lives to the service of God, and Chester retains one of the most complete sets of monastic buildings in the country. Its roots, however, are older still. We know that a Saxon church stood here before the Norman Conquest, and it may well have had a Roman predecessor – the cathedral precinct occupies one quarter of the original Roman settlement that still forms the heart of the city of Chester.

Many of the modern cathedral's most characteristic treasures reflect its medieval monastic origins, from the superb fourteenth-century quire stalls to the quirky architectural details that appear in unexpected places throughout the church and monastic buildings. Today the cathedral church is dedicated to Christ and the Blessed Virgin Mary, but the Saxon church and its Benedictine successor were both dedicated to a local Saxon saint, St Werburgh, and the medieval shrine made to hold her relics still stands in pride of place in the Lady Chapel. Having your own local saint was an important plus for a medieval church, drawing pilgrims – and business – to both church and city.

The Benedictine church, built in the soft local stone, had been extensively renovated and extended even before it became a cathedral. By the nineteenth century major restoration was necessary, and much of the immediately apparent character of the church today is the result of Victorian work, including some fine stained glass, the mosaics and the High Altar. Modern contributions include more excellent glass and the Song School, the first major new building since the Reformation. Through all these developments and changes, the spiritual life of this great building has been serenely maintained.

ABOVE This plump character, dating from the twelfth or thirteenth century, decorates one of the doorways in the cloister.

OPPOSITE One of the 48 decorative seat carvings or misericords in the quire, this one showing a formidable woman beating her unhappy husband.

ROMAN CITY AND SAXON SAINT

Chester's commanding position on the edge of a sandstone ridge, close to the much-contested Welsh borderlands and with the river Dee curving defensively around it on three sides, has ensured it a lively history. The Romans established a major military centre here only 30 years after they first invaded Britain in 43AD. The street layout reflects the Roman rectangular grid pattern, with Eastgate, Watergate, Bridge Street and Northgate forming a central cross, which now looks off-kilter as the city centre was later enlarged to south and west. The surviving medieval city wall, the most complete circuit in Britain, still follows the line of the Roman fortifications on the north and east sides.

In 313AD the Emperor Constantine extended toleration to Christians, and in 380 Christianity became the state religion of Rome under Theodosius I. There will undoubtedly have been at least one church in the city at that time, but no trace of it has been found. Tradition has it that there had been a Roman temple to Apollo on the cathedral site, which might well have been replaced in the later empire period by a church. According to a medieval source Wulfhere, Saxon king of Mercia, dedicated a church here to Sts Peter and Paul in around 660. The first reliable record we have of the building that was to become the cathedral, however, is in the early tenth century, when the relics of St Werburgh were brought to Chester to escape the Viking invaders. The Mercian queen Aethelflaed, daughter of Alfred the Great, rededicated the church of Sts Peter and Paul to St Werburgh, staffed by a college of non-resident priests known as secular canons. It was Aethelflaed, too, who refortified the old Roman walls, and possibly under her rule that they were extended to the south and west.

So who was Werburgh? A Mercian princess and Wulfhere's daughter, she renounced her royal status and joined the abbey of Ely in around 675, becoming so renowned for her virtue and piety that she was put in charge of all the nunneries in Mercia. Miracles were reported at her burial, at Hanbury in Staffordshire, and her tomb soon became a site of pilgrimage. When a Danish army threatened the area in the late ninth century from their base in York, her remains were transferred to Chester for safety, and a royal charter of 958 records a grant of land to support a *'familia'*, a community, 'serving Almighty God in honour of holy Werburgh ever virgin'.

ST WERBURGH

St Werburgh, patron saint of the city of Chester and its Benedictine monastery, is celebrated in many guises in the cathedral. Her earliest appearance is in the fourteenth-century quire stalls, where one of the wooden misericords (carved ledges to support standing monks) tells the story of her most famous miracle of the goose; when one of Werburgh's tame flock of geese is cooked and eaten by a servant and the remaining geese come to Werburgh for amends, she retrieves the bones and restores the goose to life. She appears on a boss in the vaulted ceiling of the abbey gateway, smiling benignly on visitors, and also features in several of the windows, most recently in the Great West Window of 1961. In the Brocklehurst window in the south transept, she stands by her abbey church as Christ rises to glory above her, and in the cloister windows she is shown in full Victorian nun's robes.

ABOVE RIGHT
The miracle of St Werburgh and the goose, carved on one of the misericords (decorated seats) in the quire.

BELOW NEAR RIGHT
The saint portrayed as a nineteenth-century nun, in the early twentieth-century window glass in the cloisters.

BELOW FAR RIGHT
Werburgh as shown in the modern Brocklehurst window in the south transept.

OPPOSITE A decorated boss in the ceiling of the fourteenth-century abbey gateway shows Werburgh in medieval nun's garb.

SAINT WERBURGA

ST WERBURGH

BENEDICTINE ABBEY

The Norman invasion of 1066 transformed the kingdom of England, bringing Norman rule, the French language and continental monasticism, but the northern shires put up fierce resistance long after the battle of Hastings. Chester was the very last English city to fall to the conquering William in 1070 and paid a high price; *Domesday Book* of 1086 records that the city 'had been greatly wasted', but adds 'the church of St Werburgh has 13 houses quit of every customary due', one belonging to the church warden, the others to the canons, suggesting that the monastery and church survived relatively unscathed.

To keep the area at heel, William appointed his nephew Hugh, called '*Lupus*', the wolf, as earl of Chester, one of three new earldoms on the Welsh marches with almost regal powers and responsibilities. Wolflike he may have been but Hugh, like most of his contemporaries, was also devout. He had already founded two Benedictine abbeys in Normandy, and in 1092 he reconstituted the church dedicated to St Werburgh as a Benedictine abbey, endowing it handsomely. He invited the theologian and philosopher Anselm, shortly to be installed as archbishop of Canterbury, to supervise its transformation, but retained its dedication to the Saxon saint – clearly Werburgh's reputation for miracle-working still resonated.

The north nave wall and north transept are all that remain today of Hugh Lupus's church, as it was rebuilt from the late thirteenth-century onwards, but we know that construction began at the east end and that the nave was roughly the same size as it is today. The north transept, with its round-headed internal arch and simple Romanesque triforium above, shows us what the Norman church would have looked like, but the impressively surviving abbey buildings give us a vivid sense of life in a medieval monastery. Unlike the canons of the Saxon church, living in houses in the town, Benedictine monks lived an enclosed life behind their great gateway in Northgate Street. The elegant Georgian space of Abbey Square was once the monastery's Great Court, housing lodgings for visitors, and domestic buildings such as the brewhouse and storehouse **34**.

The cloister, where those monks who could write would copy sacred texts by the unglazed window openings, and the thirteenth-century refectory (now appropriately housing the café), where they ate their meals in silence, survive largely unchanged. The

OPPOSITE The ornate south-west porch leading into the south nave was one of the latest additions to the Benedictine monastery, made in the sixteenth century, not long before the dissolution.

ABOVE Decorative boss in the north cloister walkway.

mid-thirteenth-century chapter house, an impressively dignified space in which the abbot heard pleas and conducted the day-to-day business of the monastery, was constructed in the newly fashionable Gothic style, with pointed arches and ribbed vaults, and it seems that the fashion-conscious monks then decided to rebuild the whole church in the same style. They started with the Lady Chapel in around 1270, followed by the remodelling of the quire in about 1290, but the rebuild dragged on for nearly 200 years, with the north side of the nave not completed until around 1490, and the west front and south-west porch not until the early sixteenth century.

Some of the texts produced by the monks of St Werburgh were works of considerable originality and the monastery was clearly a notable intellectual centre. In 1194 the monk Lucian wrote an extraordinary panegyric *De Laude Cestre*, 'In Praise of Chester', in which he portrayed the city in idealized terms as a cross. Ranulph Higden wrote a universal history, his *Polychronicon*, in the abbey in the first half of the fourteenth century, which seems to have had considerable success, as more than a hundred copies survive; one theory is that he was also responsible for the Chester cycle of mystery plays, which are still performed today and probably originated within the monastery. And in the early sixteenth century another monk, Henry Bradshaw, wrote a *Life of St Werburgh* in English and in ballad form, which is the source for most of what we know about the saint. It survives in print as well as manuscript and may well have been a canny move by the abbey to promote itself as a venerable and worthy institution in the face of Cardinal Wolsey's proposed reforms.

RIGHT The graceful thirteenth-century chapter house was the first addition to the monastery in the Gothic style. The window glass is by the nineteenth-century firm of Heaton, Butler & Bayne and shows scenes from the history of the building.

HENRY VIII'S CATHEDRAL CHURCH, DECLINE AND RESTORATION

In the event Wolsey's policies did not serve King Henry VIII's purpose, and his disgrace was soon followed by the far more radical total dissolution of religious houses. The abbey of St Werburgh was closed in 1539, before the planned vaulted stone ceilings could be installed. But it suffered much less damage than most, as the abbey church became the cathedral church of a new bishopric of Chester, created by subdividing the vast Lichfield diocese. On 26 July 1541, therefore, St Werburgh's was formally reconstituted as 'the Cathedral Church of Christ and the Blessed Virgin Mary in Chester', with ten of the monks staying comfortably on as cathedral staff, including Abbot John Clarke, who became dean, and Prior Nicholas Buckley, who became prebendary and survived right through the religious fluctuations of Protestant Edward VI and Catholic Mary, into the reign of Elizabeth I.

The Civil War of 1642–51 saw greater upheaval, with parliamentary troops smashing all the medieval glass and damaging the quire and St Werburgh's shrine. The effect of wind, weather and the passing of time on the soft and friable local stone was more significant still, however, and by the early nineteenth century the church was badly neglected. Major repair programmes were undertaken in 1819 and 1843–48, focusing mainly on the interior and the windows. When the noted Victorian restorer and architect George Gilbert Scott became involved in the 1850s, he condemned the exterior stonework as 'so horribly and lamentably decayed as to reduce it to a mere wreck, like a mouldering sandstone cliff'. He later became sole cathedral architect, leading an extensive restoration in 1868–76, which transformed the building both inside and out, but also secured its future.

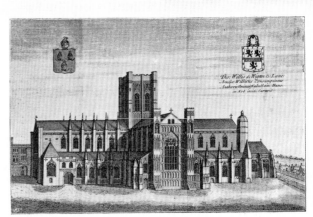

THE CATHEDRAL AT THE END OF THE SEVENTEENTH CENTURY (FROM AN OLD ENGRAVING).

LEFT This detail from the nineteenth-century chapter house window shows Henry VIII signing the royal warrant creating the see of Chester.

ABOVE Seventeenth-century engraving showing the cathedral before Victorian restoration substantially altered its external appearance.

Exterior and entrance

TODAY THE ENCLOSED AND PRIVATE WORLD OF THE MONASTERY HAS LONG since been abandoned and the cathedral opens its arms to the world – literally so, surrounded as it is to south, east and north by welcoming gardens, which once served as a graveyard. A memorial garden dedicated to the 22nd (Cheshire) Regiment occupies the area nearest to the new Bell Tower **36**, which was opened in 1975 and is the first free-standing cathedral bell tower since the fifteenth century. The city wall walk encircles the cathedral precinct to the east and north, offering panoramic views across the whole building complex.

From the outside the medieval church building looks remarkably Victorian, largely due to Scott's work. With the full support of the dean and chapter, he added parapets to the Lady Chapel, quire and quire aisles; placed pinnacles at the east end, and turrets at the west end; and topped the late-fourteenth-century crossing tower with yet more turrets, large enough to balance a spire that was never built. The flying buttresses supporting the nave and south transept are Scott's, as is the semi-circular chapel with a high cone-shaped roof that ends the south quire aisle. The 'mouldering sandstone cliff' that Scott described was refaced in Runcorn sandstone, which gives the cathedral building a neater and rather more muted

ABOVE View of the tower and south transept, taken across the military memorial garden. The turrets and parapets were added are part of George Gilbert Scott's nineteenth-century restoration.

RIGHT The west end of the cathedral was not completed until the fifteenth century; the turrets and battlements were added by Scott.

appearance than the richly red weather-worn tone and subtly eroded shapes of the stone in unrestored areas such as the abbey gateway.

When the abbey was founded, the town already pressed close up to the church on the south and so the monastic buildings were placed, unusually, on the colder north side. The visitor can walk round the east end through the gardens to what was once the abbey green, to get a view of the chapter house, the refectory and the new Song School, a brilliantly achieved modern addition to the east range of the cloister where the monks' dormitory once stood.

The western entrance to the abbey church was used only for feast days, and groups of pilgrims would more usually have entered through the two-storey south-west porch. The modern entrance to the cathedral **1** is to the left of the great west door and leads down a winding passage into the undercroft, a fine low-vaulted space with circular columns which is part of the original twelfth-century monastery. The monks would have used this for storage, while above it was once the abbot's hall, his private lodging. Today the undercroft houses the visitors' reception area and the cathedral shop, with a passage leading the visitor out into the cloisters and, from there, into the nave through one of the processional doorways.

West Entrance of the Cathedral.

FAR LEFT Early nineteenth-century print showing the west front before Scott's alterations.

LEFT Looking across the war memorial gardens to the monumental south transept.

BELOW LEFT The modern Song School on the left is built in sandstone and with lancet-style windows to blend with the thirteenth-century refectory at right.

Nave

THE NAVE **4** IS THE LARGEST AREA OF THE CATHEDRAL, THE LONG ARM OF the cross, and the only part to which laypeople would have had access when the building was still an abbey. A substantial screen would once have separated it from the east end and the High Altar, where the monks worshipped and prayed. It was only in the nineteenth century that church liturgy changed to permit a more open view. Today the nave is used not only for the principal church services, but also for a wide variety of secular celebrations, from concerts and art exhibitions to university graduation ceremonies.

It was also the last part of the earlier church to be rebuilt, in the major reconstruction that began at the east end c.1270. The earlier Norman nave seems to have been much the same size and had a west front with two squat towers; the lower stages of the north-west tower survive in what is now the baptistery. The Gothic-style rebuild of the nave seems to have begun, logically enough, with the eastern part closest to the crossing, where the first nave arch is slightly narrower than the rest. The rest of the south side of the nave is probably mid-fourteenth century, the north side possibly as much as a century later, though unusually it is built in much the same style – a surprising feature at a time when builders built what and where they chose, with little regard to any earlier designs.

The monastery was dissolved before the upper windows had been completed, while the planned stone-vaulted roof had not even been begun. The ribbed ceiling seen today was

OPPOSITE Looking east up the nave towards the quire and Lady Chapel.

LEFT The impressively ribbed nave ceiling was designed and installed as part of the nineteenth-century restoration.

designed and installed by Scott, based on local medieval examples and richly decorated with carved and gilded bosses. He used wood rather than stone in order to place less stress on the medieval walls. The series of dramatic Old Testament scenes on the wall of the north nave aisle **5**, which illustrate scenes from the lives of Abraham, Moses, Elijah and David, date from the same period. They are true mosaic, made from coloured marble rather than ceramic, and are designed in the expressive Pre-Raphaelite style. The sequence of small angel windows above the mosaics are also nineteenth-century and were created by the stained-glass design and manufacturing company of Heaton, Butler & Bayne, which was particularly famed for its Gothic Revival work.

The nave also contains some fine modern glass. The great west window **6**, designed by W.T. Carter Shapland, dates from 1961 and shows the Virgin Mary and Joseph surrounded by local saints, including Chad, Queen Aethelflaeda and, of course, Werburgh herself. Three windows in the south aisle, donated by the sixth Duke of Westminster to mark the cathedral's ninth centenary in 1992, also contain modern glass representing the contrasting themes of change and continuity.

ABOVE Detail from the nineteenth-century nave mosaics; David presents the head of the giant Goliath to Saul.

RIGHT The cathedral as arts venue; a concert given in the nave in April 2016 by the Chester Philharmonic.

All is not solemnity here, however, for the nave also contains some quirky medieval carving. High up on the north wall in the main body of the nave, at the corner of a window, is the Chester Imp, a stone carving of the Devil, kneeling and in chains. He can be found at the bottom right-hand corner of the second upper window on the north side (the left side, facing the altar). Tradition has it that a monk walking along the gallery up here saw the Devil peering in at a window, and the abbot had the carving set up to warn what would happen if he tried to enter. Equally evocative is the gamesboard cut into the right-hand pillar base at the entrance to the baptistery, at the north-west end of the nave. The game is Nine Men's Morris, similar to the modern game of Ludo – it is tempting to imagine it carved by a bored young novice monk during a long service. Monastic life offered a relatively safe, if disciplined, existence, but not everyone entered a monastery voluntarily.

FAR LEFT One of the Westminster windows in the south nave aisle.

LEFT The Chester Imp, a representation of the devil in chains carved high on the north nave wall.

BELOW LEFT Gamesboard, a medieval form of Ludo, carved into a pillar-base at the entrance to the baptistery.

THE CATHEDRAL'S STAINED GLASS

The cathedral's medieval stained glass was almost entirely destroyed during the sixteenth-century Reformation and the seventeenth-century Civil War, when representations of Christ or of any biblical scenes or characters were condemned as idolatrous. Much of the glass seen today is nineteenth century, including the striking Nativity scene in St Werburgh's chapel in the north quire aisle and the Lady Chapel windows by William Wailes, showing the Acts of the Apostles. More modern glass includes the lovely angel window in the south transept, by J.W. Brown for Powells, 1921, the great west window, 1961, and the magnificent Creation window in the refectory.

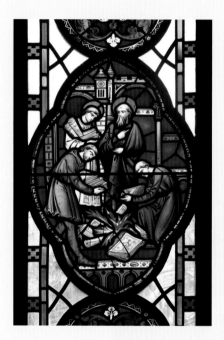

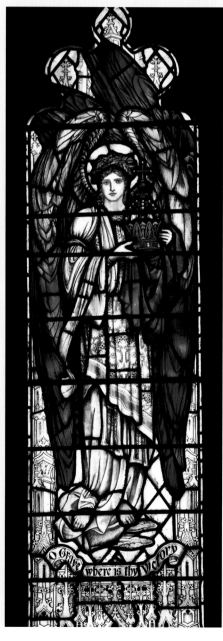

ABOVE Detail from the window glass in the Lady Chapel showing the Acts of the Apostles.

RIGHT A twentieth-century angel in Pre-Raphaelite style, from a window in the south transept.

ABOVE St James the Great with his pilgrim hat and cockle shell, from the early twentieth-century glass in the cloister.

OPPOSITE The Creation window in the refectory, dating from 2001, gives a colourful modern interpretation of the six days of creation.

AND GOD SAW EVERY THING THAT HE HAD MADE AND BEHOLD IT WAS VERY GOOD

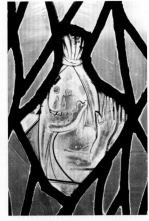

OPPOSITE The great
west window, showing
the Virgin Mary
surrounded by local
saints, including
St Werburgh on
the far left. It was
designed by W.T.
Carter Shapland and
installed in 1961.

ABOVE RIGHT The
Nativity window in
St Werburgh's chapel
has an unusually
flowing design for
nineteenth-century
glass, with the stable
roof arching across the
five medieval lancet
windows.

BELOW RIGHT These
musical angels can be
found in the north
nave aisle, above
the series of Old
Testament mosaics,
and date from the
nineteenth-century
restoration.

ABOVE One of the few
surviving fragments
of Chester's medieval
glass, this small and
macabre piece shows
a resurrected soul on
the Day of Judgement,
still wearing its
shroud. It can be
found in the quire, set
into the back of one
of the sedilia, seats for
the clergy.

BAPTISTERY AND ST ANSELM'S CHAPEL

The baptistery **2** forms the base of one of the two towers that flanked the west front of Hugh Lupus's church. This, the north-west tower, is one of the oldest surviving parts of the cathedral, retaining its Romanesque-style round arches and Norman masonry.

The font was the gift of a local nobleman, Lord Egerton of Tatton, who acquired it in Venice in 1885. It was once thought to be an early Christian survival but is now regarded as a nineteenth-century pastiche. Its decoration reflects characteristic early Christian symbolism, with the two peacocks representing the promise of eternal life, the twining vine pattern reflecting the biblical parable of Christ as a vine, and the central motif consisting of the Greek letters Chi and Rho, for Christ, and Alpha and Omega, beginning and end.

From the baptistery a winding stair leads up to one of the cathedral's more unusual treasures, only recently opened to the public. The chapel of St Anselm was built as the abbot's private place of prayer, connected to the original abbot's hall. When the abbot's hall was replaced with a bishop's palace in the seventeenth century, the chapel was made over for the bishop in an early example of Gothic Revival style, with a richly-patterned and vaulted seventeenth-century plasterwork ceiling which springs neatly from the medieval pillars. At the same time the window opening at the far end was remade as an arch, and the small square chancel was added, slightly offset because it sits over the south-west corner of the cloister. It too has a fine plasterwork ceiling, this time geometrically-patterned and enlivened with cherubs and feathers. A recess held a comfortable seat for the bishop, while a window gave him a view down to the north aisle of the nave.

ABOVE The decoration on the font reflects early Christian symbolism, the central motif combining the Greek letters Chi and Rho, for Christ, and Alpha and Omega, the beginning and the end.

LEFT The baptistery has always been a place of great solemnity, where new-born infants are welcomed into the Christian community. It is one of the earliest surviving parts of the cathedral, dating from the first Norman church and retaining its round Romanesque arches.

OPPOSITE The abbot's private place of prayer is reached today by a stair from the baptistery. It was renovated in the seventeenth century for the bishop, in an early example of Gothic Revival style.

CONSISTORY COURT

The base of the south-west tower on the south side of the west entrance offers another of Chester's unique pleasures. It houses the consistory court **3**, the earliest surviving example of the system of church courts set up after the Norman Conquest, which once had total jurisdiction over all ecclesiastical matters and continued in use until the mid-nineteenth century. Accusations of heresy, defamation or witchcraft were all heard at the consistory court, and the most notorious case here was in 1555, during the reign of the Catholic Mary, when George Marsh was tried for heresy and burnt at the stake because he would not recant his Protestant faith. Defamation was a more common charge; in 1664 Maria Williams was fined for libel for calling Elizabeth Sutton a 'rotten queane [whore] and her son a lousy bastard'. Most cases were less emotive, however, mainly involving legal work such as wills and probate or fines for failure to attend church.

This involved a vast amount of correspondence and the huge table, dating to around 1600, was designed to accommodate piles of paper, with a raised seat in the corner allowing the administrator, called the apparitor, literally to oversee the operation. The chancellor of the diocese was in overall control and sat in the central raised seat. The canopy above it, carrying the arms of the see of Chester and the wolf's head badge of Hugh Lupus, was altered to fit when the court was moved in 1636 from its original position in the Lady Chapel. Part of the name of the then chancellor, Edward Mainwaring, is missing.

OPPOSITE The consistory court at the base of the south-west tower is the only surviving old church court in England.

ABOVE LEFT The typically Renaissance screen over the entrance to the consistory court bears the date of the court's installation in this location, 1636, and forms a striking contrast with the sober atmosphere within.

Crossing and transepts

THE CROSSING **10** IS THE HEART OF THE CHURCH, WHERE THE FOUR GREAT
branches of the cruciform building meet. The original Norman structure seems to have been
replaced immediately after the quire was completed, in the 1330s. The crossing arches were
then reinforced in the 1380s to support a bell-frame with tower above. This reinforcement
takes the unusual form of smaller paired arches set above the main arches on each side of
the crossing square, with two much larger arches springing between the pairs to intersect
the great crossing space, creating a 'crown of stone' to support the weight of bells and tower
above. The cathedral bells hung in the old tower until the late 1960s, when it was found
that, despite the best efforts of the medieval masons, their combined weight had caused
structural problems over the course of 600 years and they were moved to the new free-
standing tower. The rich gold of the modern ceiling decoration contrasts effectively with the
darker masonry. It was designed by George Pace, also architect of the modern bell tower, and
installed in 1973.

In the abbey church the entrance to the quire was blocked by a great stone screen. In
keeping with the more inclusive emphasis of nineteenth-century liturgy, George Gilbert Scott
instead designed the open wooden screen seen today, both to permit a clear view from one
end of the cathedral to the other and to echo the warm medieval woodwork in the quire.

He also designed the ornate mosaic floor of the crossing and the impressive organ
loft which fills the north arch of the crossing. This stands on yellow columns which are
apparently marble but are in fact hollow, with supporting iron girders inside and the outside
coating made of *scagliola*, an ingenious composite. The organ loft was donated by the first
Duke of Westminster and bears a number of family coats of arms. The family name of the

ABOVE Chester
Philharmonic perform
in the crossing for an
audience seated in the
nave.

OPPOSITE ABOVE The
crown of stone in the
crossing, designed
to support the tower
above, contrasts with
the rich texture of the
modern ceiling.

OPPOSITE BELOW LEFT
George Gilbert Scott's
delicate wooden screen
separates the crossing
from the quire.

OPPOSITE BELOW RIGHT
Scott's quire screen is
intended to echo the
rich woodwork of the
medieval quire stalls.

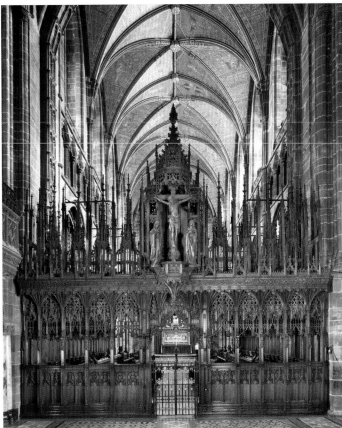

THEIR MISSING HANDS WERE ORIGINALLY JOINED IN PRAYER BUT WERE DESTROYED DURING THE CIVIL WAR BY PARLIAMENTARY TROOPS, WHO REGARDED THE PRAYING GESTURE AS A SYMBOL OF IDOLATRY.

ABOVE The fine memorial to Thomas Greene and his two wives, set into one of the piers of the crossing.

dukes of Westminster is Grosvenor and they are descended from Hugh Lupus's nephew, who also came to England in 1066 with William the Conqueror, and was known as Gilbert '*le gros veneur*', the chief huntsman.

The magnificent organ **11** dates from 1876 and was built by the newly-established local firm of Charles Whiteley & Co. It is still used almost daily to accompany services and choral evensong. The cathedral also hosts one of the most extensive series of organ recitals in the country, with a weekly Thursday recital throughout the year. The cathedral's own organists, their names recorded in an unbroken line from 1541 when the cathedral was established, perform regularly here, as do recitalists from all over the world.

On the south-west crossing pier is a colourful memorial to Thomas Greene **12**, who died in 1602, and his two wives, all wearing fine ruffs. Their missing hands were originally joined in prayer but were destroyed during the Civil War by parliamentary troops, who regarded the praying gesture as a symbol of idolatry.

NORTH TRANSEPT

FAR RIGHT Detail from the carved narwhal tusk used as a processional cross, displayed in the north transept.

BELOW NEAR RIGHT Romanesque round arch in the north transept; the later arch leading into the quire aisle has been cut through the earlier wall.

BELOW FAR RIGHT The tiny cobweb picture, showing the Virgin and Child.

The north transept **20**, now rather full of nineteenth-century memorials, gives us the clearest sense of what Hugh Lupus's Romanesque church would have looked like. It was lower than the present building, with the ceiling probably at today's gallery-level, and much darker, as the three small blocked-up openings in the left-hand (west) wall were the original windows. The simple, stepped, round arch in the right-hand (east) wall is characteristic of Romanesque style and probably dates to around 1100, almost immediately after the Benedictine monastery was founded, as does the equally austere arcade above it. The small columns are recycled Roman work dating from the first century. Immediately to the right of these, the fourteenth-century Gothic arch that leads into the north quire aisle, part of the later reconstruction of the abbey church, cuts ruthlessly through the earlier building with little attempt to hide the break in the masonry.

In a niche between the two arches is one of the cathedral's more unusual treasures, the little 'cobweb picture' **21** of the Virgin Mary and Child, which is painted on a treated web of caterpillar's silk. The tradition began in the Innsbruck area of Austria, where this nineteenth-century example was probably made, as it is a copy of a painting by Lucas Cranach the Elder in the cathedral in Innsbruck. On the opposite side of the transept, mounted on the wall, is a 2-metre-long carved narwhal's tusk, surmounted by a cross so that it could be used as a processional cross. The narwhal is an unusual Arctic whale with a single long tooth or horn.

The walls of the transept were heightened in the fifteenth century, when the nave was still being finished, and the impressive camber-beam roof was installed in about 1520, only 20 years before the monastery became a cathedral. Among the many richly-decorated ceiling bosses are the arms of both Henry VIII and Cardinal Wolsey.

THE CATHEDRAL'S MOSAICS

Chester Cathedral contains some magnificent examples of nineteenth-century mosaic. The floor of the crossing was designed by George Gilbert Scott as part of his major restoration of the building in 1868–76. In St Erasmus's Chapel in the south quire aisle, the mosaic on the altar wall was made in 1879 in honour of Thomas Brassey, extraordinary builder of railways, who by 1847 had made almost one-third of the railways in Britain, and by the time of his death in 1870 was responsible for one in every twenty miles of railway in the world. The mosaic reredos of the *Last Supper* behind the High Altar in the quire was designed by the same artist, J.R. Clayton, also of the noted Gothic Revival glass manufacturers Clayton & Bell, as was the sequence of Old Testament mosaic scenes in the nave.

OPPOSITE The pavement of the sanctuary was laid as part of the Victorian restoration of 1868–76 and consists of a sequence of medallions with portraits of the Apostles. The frames are formed of small stones, tesserae, from the site of the Temple of Jerusalem.

LEFT The sequence of nineteenth-century mosaics in the north nave aisle shows Old Testament scenes; here Pharaoh's daughter finds the infant Moses in his cradle on the banks of the river Nile.

OPPOSITE The rich inlaid floor of the crossing was designed by George Gilbert Scott and made by John Thomson & Sons in 1875–76.

LEFT Detail from the *Last Supper* reredos behind the High Altar in the quire, designed by J.R. Clayton.

SOUTH TRANSEPT

The original south transept was the same size as the one on the north, and the ground-plan of the Norman church was symmetrical. Its reconstruction in the more fashionable Gothic style did not begin until around 1350, after the quire and crossing had been transformed. By then changes in the liturgy (the form of worship), including a greater emphasis on intercessionary Masses for the souls of the dead, led the fourteenth-century monks to include four extra chapels for these Masses in their rebuild. Normally two of these would have been placed in each transept, maintaining the symmetrical ground-plan, but the north transept could not be enlarged, as the cloister and the chapter-house stood up against its external wall.

Instead the south transept **7** was reconstructed on a hugely ambitious scale, five bays long, as against just one bay on the north side, and with arcaded aisles on both sides. The eastern aisle accommodates four separate chapels, making this transept also much wider than its counterpart. This process took so long that by the time it was completed, the first phase of Gothic architecture, known as Early English, had modulated into the much more ornamental Decorated stage, which can be most clearly seen in the complex window tracery of the south window and the smaller windows in the four chapels. Almost a complete church in its own right, this large space did in fact serve a separate congregation, the parish of St Oswald, for three centuries, until 1881, and was walled off from the crossing. It is the largest transept in any English cathedral church.

The four chapels were substantially remodeled as part of the nineteenth-century restoration and now hold some fine Victorian artworks. The chapel of St Oswald has a superb reredos behind the altar, by the designer and stained-glass manufacturer Charles Kempe, who also designed the window above. It shows the seventh-century Northumbrian king and saint, Oswald, who converted to Christianity after a victory in battle. Another fine reredos in the chapel of St George shows the saint about to impale the unfortunate dragon on his spear, and was carved in pale oak to a design by Giles Gilbert Scott, grandson of George and himself cathedral architect from 1908. This chapel also holds the colours and other memorials of the 22nd Cheshire regiment, founded in 1689.

CROSSING AND TRANSEPTS | 39

THE CATHEDRAL'S MEMORIALS

The monuments in any church can offer a moving insight into the achievements and travails of the local inhabitants, testifying both to the generosity of benefactors and to the self-sacrifice of the war-dead. One of Chester's most splendid memorials, in the south transept, is to Hugh Lupus Grosvenor, who was the MP for Chester for 22 years, from 1847 to 1869, and was created first Duke of Westminster in 1874 **8**. Other smaller tributes honour the dead of many wars through the centuries, in Europe and beyond, forming a sad record of the losses endured by the local community in the service of their country.

OPPOSITE Memorial window in the cloister to George Mallory and Andrew Irvine, who died on Mount Everest in 1924. Mallory's body was finally found in 1999; it is still not known whether the two men had reached the summit before they lost their lives.

FAR LEFT ABOVE AND BELOW Details from the monumental memorial to Hugh Lupus Grosvenor, first Duke of Westminster, in the south transept. The heraldic small dog holds the ducal arms; the wheatsheaf was once the arms of the earldom of Chester.

LEFT This ornate monument at the west end of the cathedral commemorates Roger Barnston, citizen of Chester and colonel of the local militia, who died in 1842.

Quire and high altar

IF THE CROSSING IS THE ARCHITECTURAL HEART OF ANY CATHEDRAL, the quire **13** has always been its emotional and liturgical centre. Originally it also offered a sanctuary where medieval fugitives could claim immunity, whether from persecutors or from the heavy hand of secular authority. Here the Benedictine monks stood in the superb fourteenth-century choirstalls to sing their daily offices, known as the *opus dei*, God's work, and here today the principal festivals of the church calendar are still celebrated at the High Altar and Evensong is sung. Originally the fourteenth-century shrine of St Werburgh, now in the Lady Chapel, probably stood here at the east end, behind the High Altar, giving additional meaning and focus to medieval worship.

The quire was built immediately after the Lady Chapel in the east-to-west sequence replacing the Norman church, and in a rather more decorated Gothic style. It has a typical three-storey design of ground-floor arcade and upper-level clerestory, separated by a low gallery, the triforium. Like the south transept, it is five bays long. The building process seems to have been both complex and lengthy, from roughly 1270 to 1320. Recent research, based on variations in the decorative detailing, suggests the involvement of no fewer than six different master masons. Although designed to carry a stone vault, the quire was never vaulted and the fine nineteenth-century oak roof, designed by J.R. Clayton, was installed as part of George Gilbert Scott's renovations.

Even here in the sanctuary the quirky individuality of medieval stone carvers can be seen at play. In the right-hand quire arcade (as you face the altar), on two of the wall-pillars which soar up through the gallery and clerestory to support the roof, two of the masons' team have been preserved in stone. They can be seen just above the decorated capitals of the columns on either side of the bishop's throne. The figure on the left, with both arms above his head, literally holds the building up, his knees buckling with the effort, while the bearded one on the right, clearly the master mason, supports the building with his right hand while clutching the plans on his knee with his left.

OPPOSITE Detail from the richly ornamental nineteenth-century oak ceiling of the quire, which shows the angelic orchestra and Old Testament prophets.

ABOVE These two medieval masons are carved high up on the right-hand wall in the sanctuary, one struggling to hold up the ceiling, the other clutching the plan of the building.

One of the few surviving documents relating to the business affairs of the abbey gives us a clue as to why the quire took so long to build. In 1277 Edward I is recorded as undertaking that the loan of 100 workmen by the abbot for the construction of Flint Castle will not be taken as a precedent. At this time, Chester was the operational base for the king's campaign against the Welsh, which included the building of a chain of castles along the Marches, and clearly a team of experts working on a half-finished church was far too convenient to be ignored - and equally clearly the 1277 loan did indeed prove a precedent, as another document of 1282 records a similar transaction. In return, the abbey seems to have acquired a military engineer, as the final building stage in the quire, roughly 1310-20, is linked with the name 'Richard the Engineer', a castle specialist who was second-in-command to Master James of St George, the architect of the great castles built at Caernarvon, Harlech and Conway.

The appearance of the quire today, however, is as much due to its extensive reorganization by Scott in 1872–76, when the High Altar **14** itself was moved further east to stand within the arch leading to the Lady Chapel. The nineteenth-century altar, with its mid-twentieth century frame of candle-bearing angels, is made of wood imported from the Holy Land. The impressive mosiac depiction of the Last Supper behind the altar also dates from the 1870s, as does the tiled floor, richly decorated with coloured marble and images of the Passover. The nineteenth-century glass set in the east window, high above the altar, echoes the theme of divine intercession in its depiction of Christ's Presentation in the Temple, and was made by Heaton, Butler & Bayne. And, delightfully, modern craftsmen have allowed themselves to be infected with medieval quirkiness; on the inside of the wooden altar rail, slightly to the left of centre, is carved a small and charming mouse, the signature of the workshop of Robert Thompson of Kilburn, in Yorkshire.

Among surviving medieval furnishings in the quire are four ornamental seats, or sedilia, for the clergy officiating at services, which are set into the wall separating the quire from the south quire aisle. Two small rare sections of surviving medieval glass have been inserted into their frame. The towering bishop's throne or *cathedra* on the other side of the south quire aisle arch, on the other hand, is a nineteenth-century creation, designed by Scott and modelled on the central canopy of the quire screen.

OPPOSITE ABOVE The *Last Supper* mosaic behind the High Altar was designed as part of Scott's restoration by the firm of Clayton & Bell and made by Venetian mosaicist Antonio Salviati, who used gold set between two layers of glass to achieve the rich effect.

OPPOSITE BELOW The monastic quire stalls are one of the great treasures of Chester Cathedral and date from around 1380.

RIGHT The mouse carved on the inside of the wooden altar rail is the signature of a modern craftsman.

QUIRE STALLS

The cathedral's greatest treasure is the set of 48 intricately carved wooden quire stalls **15** which line both sides of the quire, one of the finest sets in the whole of England and masterpieces of the carpenter's art. They were made in around 1380 for the monks singing their daily services; the dean and chapter and honorary canons now have named stalls here, but members of the congregation can also sit here for the daily service of Evensong.

Each stall is individually carved and over each soars a high, spiky, architectural canopy, originally designed to provide some shelter from wind and weather whistling through unglazed windows. The design of the canopies, and of the stalls as a whole, is very similar to the slightly earlier ones at Lincoln and they were almost certainly made by the same team of travelling craftsmen. Here, too, Scott's hand can be seen; thin wooden columns originally ran from the armrests to the canopies, but these were removed in the 1870s and replaced by musical angels, while the stalls too were restored, and five misericords which were regarded by the then dean as indecent were replaced.

The bench-ends to each set of stalls are carved with wonderfully lively biblical and symbolic scenes. The dean's stall, nearest the quire screen on the south side, carries a fine Tree of Jesse, a standard medieval representation of the ancestry of Christ, with the Old Testament patriarch Jesse, father of David, lying at the foot; succeeding generations arranged above; culminating in the Coronation of the Virgin at the top. The armrest of this stall is a seated pilgrim, his hat and head disproportionately large for the rest of him. On the north side the vice-dean's stall-end shows the Pelican in her Piety, believed by the medieval world to sacrifice herself by piercing her breast to feed her starving children on her own blood, in a symbol of Christ's Passion. Another armrest shows a rather improbable elephant bearing a castle or armoured seat on its back – it seems most unlikely that the carver had ever seen such a creature, as he has given it horse's feet.

Even more idiosyncratic and enchanting are the little decorated ledges that protrude

OVER EACH SOARS A HIGH, SPIKY ... CANOPY, ORIGINALLY DESIGNED TO PROVIDE SOME SHELTER FROM WIND AND WEATHER WHISTLING THROUGH UNGLAZED WINDOWS.

from the underside of the hinged seats in each stall. These are 'misericords', from *misericordia*, Latin for mercy, as they allowed the weary monks to prop themselves and rest a little while still standing to sing during the long services. The underneath of each ledge is carved with a different scene, some high-mindedly spiritual, others decidedly secular. Being relatively inaccessible, they were an opportunity for light-heartedness and experiment as well as more uplifting imagery, and only five of them show biblical scenes. Like the canopies, they bear a close resemblance to their Lincoln precursors, which had been created by the same craftsmen in 1370, ten years earlier.

The medieval tradition of decorated misericords first appears in the eleventh century and was well established by the fourteenth, with certain symbolically significant scenes appearing frequently. These include the Wild Man, always shown with shaggy beard and dressed in a hairy lionskin – at Chester there are several examples, one of them shown riding a lion; the Ascent of Alexander, based on a tradition that the conquering Alexander surveyed the end of the world from a basket borne by two huge birds; and the Crafty Fox, who plays dead to trap his prey. Another very popular and evergreen subject is the Battle of the Sexes – a wife beating her husband.

A more unusual scene, also found at Lincoln, comes from the romance of Sir Yvain (Gawain), in which Yvain, pursuing another knight into his castle, is caught by the falling portcullis, which cuts his unfortunate horse in two. One scene that is unique to Chester shows the legend of St Werburgh and the geese: on one side the destructive geese are enclosed in a pen; on the right, the kneeling thief confesses to having stolen and eaten the missing bird; and in the centre, the saint reassembles the bones and resurrects the bird.

OPPOSITE One of the nineteenth-century musical angels added to the quire canopies during the Victorian restoration.

NEAR RIGHT The Tree of Jesse, carved on the end of the dean's stall, showing the descent of Christ from Old Testament patriarch Jesse.

CENTRE RIGHT The crouching figure with tankard carved on this bench-end is half-man, half-goat.

FAR RIGHT One of the more unusual of the misericords shows a horse caught by a falling portcullis.

NORTH QUIRE AISLE AND ST WERBURGH'S CHAPEL

Each of the two quire aisles is separated from the transept by a pair of magnificent iron gates, made in Spain and dated 1558, which were the gift of the first Duke of Westminster. The aisles originally ended in a semicircle aligned with the arch into the Lady Chapel. They were both extended in the sixteenth century to give access to the Lady Chapel, but only the northern extension remains, now St Werburgh's chapel.

Today the north quire aisle holds a number of interesting furnishings, including some fragments of the original medieval stone screen that separated the quire from the crossing, which were removed and placed here as part of Scott's reorganization of the quire.

Looking up the length of the aisle, the eye-catching nineteenth-century window in St Werburgh's chapel **17** at the end immediately draws attention, as it was designed to do. It shows the Nativity and was made in 1857 by the father-and-son glass manufacturing firm of Michael and Arthur O'Connor. Michael was Dublin-born and trained as a heraldic painter, which perhaps explains the unusually free and flowing design, in which the stable roof arches uninterruptedly across the five lancet windows that make up the whole, in contrast to the more typically Victorian style of the windows in the north wall. The altar in the chapel is supposed to have been constructed from a fourteenth-century wooden screen.

ABOVE A glass display case in the north quire aisle holds some of the cathedral's gold and silver treasures, including Eucharistic vessels and this bishop's crozier.

LEFT This dramatic appliqué tapestry showing the cathedral and Chester city centre hangs in the north quire aisle.

ABOVE Detail of one of the pair of seventeenth-century Spanish iron gates that separate the two quire aisles from the crossing.

OPPOSITE The chapel of St Werburgh, at the end of the north quire aisle, holds a magnificent nineteenth-century window showing the Nativity.

SOUTH QUIRE AISLE AND ST ERASMUS'S CHAPEL

The sixteenth-century chapel on the south side that matched St Werburgh's chapel on the north was removed as part of George Gilbert Scott's renovation of the exterior. At the same time, the south quire aisle was shortened and a new apsidal chapel was constructed at its end, with a controversial cone-shaped roof, in memory of the Victorian railway contractor Thomas Brassey. The result, though impressive in itself, is an awkward interruption in the easy flow of movement through the cathedral, as the Lady Chapel can now be reached only from the north quire aisle and not from the south.

St Erasmus's chapel **16** is dedicated to the patron saint of sailors, also known as St Elmo, and is set aside for private prayer. The stone vaulting, the stained glass and the mosaic behind the altar form a single symbolic scheme, designed by the firm of Clayton & Bell and representing the five virtues of Faith, Hope, Charity, Humility and Patience. A characterful bust of Thomas Brassey, who by 1847 was responsible for over a third of the railway tracks laid in Britain, stands in a niche to the left of the altar, and the mosaic reredos is inscribed as sacred to his memory. In contrast to Victorian monumentality, beyond Brassey's bust is an elaborately decorated niche with a complicated curved and pointed arch, set into the surviving medieval wall and supported on two violently struggling figures.

RIGHT This richly ornamental medieval niche on one of the side-piers rests on two bizarre and violently struggling figures, forming a striking contrast to the solemn nineteenth-century decoration of the rest of the chapel.

FAR RIGHT Bust of railway magnate Thomas Brassey, who is commemorated in the chapel's mosaic.

OPPOSITE The decoration in the chapel of St Erasmus in the south quire aisle dates from the Victorian restoration; the walls, ceiling and window form a single decorative scheme.

Lady Chapel

STANDING BEYOND THE QUIRE AT THE EAST END OF THE CATHEDRAL, the Lady Chapel **18** was the first part of the monastery's new Gothic church to be built, in around 1260–80, though considerably altered during Scott's restoration. It extends east beyond the end of the original Norman church and was inspired by the Gothic style of the recently completed chapter house. Dedicated to the Virgin Mary at a time when the cult of the Virgin was at its height, it is one of many such additions made to church buildings at the time. The monks met here every day to celebrate the 'Lady Mass', and it is still used for smaller services today.

What is immediately striking about the chapel now is its dramatic use of contrasting colour, which dates only from 1969 but is based on known historical examples and gives a vivid sense of just how rich and colourful the medieval church would have been. The otherwise relatively austere design of the Lady Chapel is typical of the first phase of medieval Gothic building, known as Early English, with tall, thin lancet windows, and decorative vaulting shafts that rise from the floor and curve into ribs, whose intersections are marked by ornate bosses.

The three largest central bosses are peopled with figures representing (from the east end) the Trinity, the Virgin and Child with angels, and the murder of Thomas Becket. This last took place in Canterbury Cathedral in 1170, just over 100 years earlier, and gave rise to a cult of martyrdom that proved hugely profitable to Canterbury in attracting pilgrimage, no doubt prompting other monastic houses to hope for something similar.

To the right of the altar, set into the wall in decorative niches, are a piscina, a shallow basin used for cleansing the Eucharistic vessels, and sedilia, seats for the clergy conducting the service. The window glass is all by the Newcastle firm of William Wailes, another well-known and successful stained-glass manufacturer, and was installed in 1871 to a plan by the then dean showing the Acts of the Apostles, while the charming modern statue of Mary guiding the infant Jesus's first steps was made in 1999 by Harold Gosney.

OPPOSITE The rich colour of the Lady Chapel is based on historical examples. The modern statue on the left shows Mary guiding the infant Jesus.

FAR LEFT Decorative niches in the Lady Chapel wall; one would have held a basin for water, the other served as seats for the clergy.

NEAR LEFT This ceiling boss gives a graphic depiction of the murder of Thomas Becket.

THE SHRINE OF ST WERBURGH

At the west end of the Lady Chapel, near where the visitor enters it today, stands the shrine of St Werburgh **19**, made as a monumental resting place and display piece for the relics of Chester's very own Saxon saint. Pilgrimage was extremely popular in medieval England, spurred on by the murder of Thomas Becket in 1170 at Canterbury, and churches with their own martyred local saint were quick to exploit the trend, as pilgrims brought valued business both to monastery and to town.

Dating from about 1340, St Werburgh's shrine would originally have stood at the east end of the quire. Pilgrims would visit the shrine via the quire aisles on each side, as they were not permitted to enter the monastic space. The shrine looks like a two-storey miniature chapel and is richly decorated in a mock-architectural style. The lower level consists of six pointed-arch niches, two on each side and one at each end, each with mock vaulting. Kneeling worshippers could tuck their heads into these recesses as they voiced their petitions to Werburgh, and a fascinating recent experiment has found that the recesses are powerful amplifiers and echo-chambers, giving the praying pilgrim the sense of an intimate encounter with the saint. The upper level, which housed the relics, has window-type openings on each side, sumptuously decorated with tracery, and topped by traceried buttresses adorned with gilded statuettes of saints, each with its own ornamental canopy. Today a charming modern statuette of Werburgh and her goose stands here.

Here too the medieval mason asserted his individuality – on one corner of the shrine, positioned at the junction of the two storeys, is a little dog, much worn by the years, but still clearly cocking its leg to scratch an itchy ear. It reminded the viewer that everything in the world, both high and low, belonged to God and had a place in his house – even a small dog and his fleas!

For the remaining two centuries of the abbey church's existence the shrine must have remained the beating heart of the abbey, but at the Reformation the saint's remains were removed and the shrine was taken apart, although the relics were apparently buried nearby. In 1635 the base and part of the upper section was adapted to make the bishop's throne; further missing sections were found in 1873; and in 1888 the shrine was reassembled and placed in the Lady Chapel.

OPPOSITE
St Werburgh's shrine was made as a magnificent receptacle to hold the saint's remains and to serve as a magnet for pilgrims.

FAR LEFT
A modern statuette of the saint and her goose now stands in the shrine.

NEAR LEFT
This irreverent little dog having a good scratch is part of the original decoration of the shrine.

RIGHT ABOVE The
magnificent vaulted
undercroft, once a
storage space, today
houses the cathedral
shop.

RIGHT BELOW The
falconry in the Dean's
Field is a new and
popular attraction.

Monastic precinct

ONE OF THE DELIGHTS OF CHESTER IS ITS SUBSTANTIALLY COMPLETE MONASTIC quarter, set in a relatively secluded area to the north of the cathedral, and enclosed to the north and east by the city wall. Normally the cloister **22**, where the monks worked on their writing and copying tasks, would be on the south side of the church, to take advantage of light and warmth, but the town and graveyard already filled this space when the Normans began to build.

Clustered around the cloister garth are the undercroft, now housing visitor reception and the cathedral shop but once a storage space sited beneath the abbot's hall; the chapter house and its vestibule; and the refectory, today again serving as a refreshment place, the cathedral café. Abbey Square is further to the north, now a calm residential enclave but still entered from Northgate by the original abbey gateway, while Abbey Street leads away from the square towards a postern gate which once gave access to the abbey kaleyard, the monks' vegetable garden beyond the walls. To the left of the postern is the entrance to the Dean's Field, a large open space and the cathedral's nature garden. It also now houses a falconry, where expert falconers give demonstrations of the extraordinary skills of these powerful birds.

OPPOSITE, CLOCKWISE
FROM TOP LEFT This
decorative doorway
and window, probably
dating from the late
twelfth century, give
access to the monk's
day stair, which now
leads to the Song
School.

The cloister has
many entrances
leading off it, each
one in a different
style.

This vaulted
passageway, known as
the slype, once led out
to the abbey green.

Looking from the
slype into the east
cloister walkway.

CLOISTERS AND CLOISTER GARTH

Monastic cloisters consist of a square of covered and arcaded walkways surrounding an open space. These walkways were at the centre of day-to-day monastic life, and still offer today's visitors their first experience of the abbey buildings from the visitor centre in the undercroft. A cloister was built here when the monastery was first established in the late eleventh century and the structure today is a complex mixture of dates and styles. The roofs date from the 1530s, while that of the south cloister walk is a restoration from 1913; the tracery in the windows is an early-sixteenth century form, similar to that in the nave clerestory.

The sixteenth-century reconstruction of the vaulting took little account of existing openings into the cloister, and the original doorway that led up to the abbot's hall was – and still is – ruthlessly blocked by a column added as a roofing support. The great Reformation debate was already well under way in Europe at this time, and Henry VIII's breach with the Catholic church that led to the dissolution of the monasteries had also begun – the first religious houses were closed by Thomas Cromwell in 1525 – so it seems extraordinary that the Chester monks were undertaking such a major project.

The south range, set against the north wall of the church, still retains its round-headed Romanesque arches, and the two ornate doorways which lead into the cathedral from either end of the range also date from the late eleventh century. Two groups of three tomb recesses also stand here, all slightly different and probably dating from the late twelfth century, although the small columns may date from the ninth-century church, in another example of medieval recycling. This walkway is rather wider than the others, with a row of pillars forming a series of alcoves. These served as the scriptorium, where monastic scribes sat at desks set between the pillars to catch the daylight. A surviving will from 1526 makes provision for glass in the open arcades as part of the rebuild, no doubt extremely welcome to chilly monastic fingers in the winter months.

The east walkway gives access to the chapter house through the chapter house vestibule. Beyond the chapter house entrance is a passageway known as the slype **26**, whose vaulted roof retains its rich, dark, thirteenth-century character. It was once the lay entrance and led out to the abbey green, where the infirmary and other domestic buildings stood. It is now blocked at the far end but just around the corner, invisible from the cloister, is a stained glass window from 1939 showing the monk Ranulph Higden hard at work on his history of the world, sitting in an imaginative interpretation of the alcoves in the south walk, and wearing rather improbable loafers.

Beyond the slype in the east cloister is yet another finely decorated archway, in a transitional style marking the shift from Romanesque to Gothic, and probably late twelfth century in date. Just inside it is the grand day stair **25**, tunnel-vaulted in its lower level and originally handsomely lit from the cloister by two circular window openings, though the upper one is now blocked by the later cloister vaulting. The day stair once led to the monks' dormitory, and would have been used for the first service of the day, Prime.

OPPOSITE ABOVE This shelf in the north cloister walkway is close to the refectory door and once held a water-basin so that the monks could wash their hands before eating.

OPPOSITE BELOW The row of pillars in the south walkway form a series of alcoves where the monks read and studied; the recesses in the opposite wall once held tombs.

Today the day stair leads to the new Song School, completed in January 2003 by the Shrewsbury architectural partnership of Arrol & Snell on the site of the dormitory, and providing practice rooms for the cathedral choirs, office space and storage. Built in red sandstone and roofed in blue slate to match the cathedral building, this is the first major addition to the cathedral precinct since the Reformation. It reflects the importance attached by the dean and chapter to the maintenance of the English choral tradition at Chester.

The cloisters were again rebuilt in 1871–72 as part of George Gilbert Scott's restoration, and the delightful early twentieth-century glass here represents a calendar of saints' days, starting in the north walk opposite the chapter house entrance and moving anti-clockwise. Each saint is shown with an associated building or scene, St Ethelberga with Ely Cathedral, St James the Great with his pilgrim hat, while the figures on the south-east side represent notable figures in the Church of England, including John Wesley and Bishop Cosin of Durham.

The cloister garden, known as the garth, provides a peaceful oasis in the city centre and also offers a good view of the Romanesque north transept, the fifteenth-century tower and the Song School. Today the garth is kept as a formal garden but it would originally have been a working space, growing herbs and other medicinal plants, while the deep square pool, partly set into the rock, acted as a reservoir and fish pond. The abbey water supply was piped in after 1282 from a spring at Christleton, two miles outside the city, quite a feat of engineering. The modern sculpture here, by Stephen Broadbent and installed in 1994, is called, appropriately enough, *The Water of Life* and illustrates the parable of the Samaritan woman who encounters Jesus at the well and is converted by him.

OPPOSITE ABOVE The cloister garth is a tranquil garden, set at the heart of the medieval monastery and containing the water supply.

OPPOSITE BELOW LEFT One of the two eleventh-century entrances leading from the cloister into the cathedral; the later ceiling vaulting obliterated part of its decorative arch.

OPPOSITE BELOW RIGHT Detail of the modern statue, *The Water of Life*, which stands in the centre of the garth.

LEFT Ranulph Higden, monk of Chester who wrote a history of the world, from a window in the slype.

CHAPTER HOUSE

The chapter house **28**, entered from the east cloister via a spacious vestibule, was where the monks met daily, both for readings from a chapter of the Rule of St Benedict that governed their lives (hence the building's name), and to manage the business affairs of the abbey, which owned substantial estates.

The chapter house and vestibule were the last parts of the cloister complex to be built, and were designed in the new Gothic style to reflect early-thirteenth-century taste. The vestibule **27** has a low ceiling, carried on slender piers that break up the space and open smoothly out into ribs supporting the roof vaults, with no column capitals to interrupt the graceful line. An open archway leads into the chapter house proper, with symmetrical window openings on either side, a triple arrangement that reinforces the sense of calm authority.

The chapter house, probably built immediately after the vestibule in around 1250–60, is much taller and forms a dramatic contrast. The soaring lancet windows, and the rib-vaulted ceiling supported on wall-shafts rather than free-standing columns, give the impression of an open, light-filled space. An early and magnificent example of the Early English Gothic style, it was this building that inspired the monks to begin the reconstruction of their old-fashioned Romanesque church.

The east window in the chapter house was ingeniously designed by the nineteenth-century firm of Heaton, Butler & Bayne to work within the thirteenth-century framework of five lancet windows, and tells the story of St Werburgh's abbey, from its Anglo-Saxon foundation to its re-establishment first as a Benedictine monastery and finally as an Anglican cathedral. Below the window is a rare survival, a large cabinet with gracefully decorative ironwork which has been dated to the late thirteenth century.

OPPOSITE The spacious light-filled chapter house inspired a radical rebuild of the whole abbey in the new Gothic style.

RIGHT Detail of the thirteenth-century metalwork on the chest that stands in the chapter house.

FAR RIGHT The vestibule, with its low ceiling carried on a series of piers, forms a striking contrast to the chapter house.

REFECTORY

The refectory **29**, once the monks' dining room and still in use as the cathedral restaurant, opens off the north cloister walk. An interesting survival in the cloister to the right of the refectory doorway gives us a hint as to medieval hygiene habits associated with eating; set into the wall is a three-bay opening over a ledge which would once have held a lead basin, a *lavatorium* **24**, in which the monks would wash their hands before entering to eat and again on leaving. Here again, the roof supports for later vaulting interrupt the earlier construction.

The refectory is largely late thirteenth or early fourteenth century, with the fine hammerbeam roof added in 1939, but the scalloped doorway from the cloister is Norman and there must therefore have been an earlier refectory which was replaced by the present room. Here the monks ate all their meals in silence, while one of them read suitably uplifting texts aloud from the beautiful built-in pulpit **30**, perhaps the finest surviving example in the country. This is reached by a stair running up inside the thickness of the wall, opening to the room with a series of decorated archways and lit from behind by windows into the cloister, all surviving from around 1290.

The two principal windows form a telling contrast. The early twentieth-century east window shows the Saxon monarchs and saints associated with the early history of the monastery, set in an orderly grid, with St Werburgh in the centre holding the cathedral in her hand. The west, or Creation, window **31** was installed in 2001 to celebrate the millennium and is a joyful riot of colour illustrating the six days of the Creation in the upper lights, with modern commentaries in the lower, such as the cityscape bottom left. The artist, Rosalind Grimshaw, has Parkinson's disease and the window is a wonderful tribute to her talent and determination.

The tapestry on the west wall shows a scene from the life of the apostle Paul. Its colours have darkened over time, making it hard to appreciate, but it has an interesting history. It was made at the Mortlake tapestry works in south London in the seventeenth century, after a design by the Italian High Renaissance artist Raphael. It was given to Chester by the seventeenth-century bishop John Bridgeman and originally hung behind the High Altar, to separate the sanctuary from the Lady Chapel beyond.

OPPOSITE The impressive built-in pulpit in the refectory wall, where a monk would read aloud during meals.

LEFT Detail from the refectory window, showing St Werburgh holding the church dedicated to her.

BELOW The medieval refectory, with its fine twentieth-century hammerbeam roof, today houses the cathedral café.

ABBEY GATEWAY AND ABBEY SQUARE

Today Abbey Square **32** is a quiet, cobbled, residential quarter, substantially redeveloped in the mid-eighteenth century and retaining an atmosphere of Georgian elegance, but in medieval times it was the abbey's outer courtyard, a busy space housing domestic buildings such as the guesthouse, brewery and bakehouse. By the early fourteenth century, if not before, the whole abbey enclave was enclosed within a precinct wall to the south and west, linking up with the city wall. Some of the western wall, running parallel to Northgate Street, survives behind the houses in Abbey Square, as do its two gateways, monumental Abbey Gateway leading out to Northgate Street, and Little Abbey Gateway further north.

Abbey Gateway **33** has the double entrance – one large carriageway and one smaller footway – typical of a monastic gateway. But the wide, stepped, outer archway which encloses them on the city side is much more unusual, and links the gatehouse with the chain of castles, particularly the Queen's Gate at Caernarfon, built by Edward I against the Welsh in the late thirteenth century, for which he had 'borrowed' the abbot's workmen. The style of construction is similar to the work of the mason identified as 'Richard the Engineer' in the quire, around 1320. Inside the gatehouse arch, the ridge line of the vault carries a series of characterful decorative bosses; St Werburgh in her nun's habit watches over her visitors, while two dragons curl and bite and a lion seems to doze gently.

OPPOSITE Abbey Gateway, showing its double entrance and unusual outer arch; the rich tone of the unrestored lower level contrasts with the blander tone of the rebuilt upper storey.

LEFT One of the decorative bosses inside the gateway arch, this one showing a sleeping lion with well-curled mane.

Looking to the future

SET IN THE HEART OF THE CITY, CHESTER CATHEDRAL CONTINUES TO play a vital role today and into the future, both within the local community and on the wider modern stage, offering a sacred space for people of all faiths and none, a tranquil environment and a warm welcome to visitors. It is not only a centre for worship, but also a focus for charitable causes, an educational institution, and a vibrant musical community, serving as a unique venue for large-scale functions and hospitality.

Music has always been central to the English Christian tradition, from the plainchant of the medieval monks in their quire stalls to the inspirational compositions of today's composers, and the choral tradition remains at the heart of Chester's musical life, with the new Song School providing modern facilities. The Nave Choir, a professional-standard mixed-voice choir, is the longest-serving voluntary cathedral choir in the country and sings regularly for services in the cathedral, including the weekly service of Compline at 6:30pm on Sundays. The Cathedral Choir, with choristers drawn entirely from schools in the area, sings most days in the cathedral, broadcasts regularly on television and radio, performs at least three concerts a year and undertakes tours to other countries. The fine nineteenth-century organ is also in regular use, with weekly organ recitals by visitors from all over the world as well as by the cathedral's own organists.

ABOVE The cathedral is full of angels.

RIGHT the magnificent organ-loft, set into an arch of the crossing.

Education is also a major part of the cathedral's mission, and the education department welcomes thousands of children and young people every year for interactive tours and educational activities, with tours and workshops tailored to suit all age ranges from Key Stage 1 to A-level.

Non-school activities include foreign-language tours and organized visits for uniformed organizations and other specialist groups. Group tours available include a full cathedral tour, a 'top ten' tour focusing on the features not to be missed, a highlights tour and a tower tour offering panoramic views from the roof.

The cathedral building serves regularly as a gallery and exhibition space, with the great space of the south transept in particular often filled with an eye-catching temporary display of art, whether by established artists or by local schoolchildren inspired by the monastic spaces they have visited.

Cathedrals are not only ancient institutions, with venerable traditions; they are also living, growing, changing communities. Chester Cathedral looks constantly to the future, working to anticipate, absorb and reflect the rapid pace of the modern world, and finding fresh ways to reach out into the wider community and communicate the fundamental Christian message of faith and hope.

FAR LEFT
A Remembrance Day service fills the crossing and nave.

LEFT ABOVE
HRH the Prince of Wales and the Duchess of Cornwall visit the cathedral in 2014.

LEFT BELOW
The installation in Chester Cathedral in March 2015 of Libby Lane as bishop of Stockport, the UK's first female bishop.

Text by Jessica Hodge © Chester Cathedral 2017
Original ground plan by Martin Lubikowski,
adapted by Cedric Knight,
© Chester Cathedral 2017

First published in 2017 by
Scala Arts & Heritage Publishers Ltd
10 Lion Yard, Tremadoc Road,
London sw4 7nq, UK
www.scalapublishers.com

In association with Chester Cathedral

ISBN 978-1-78551-079-3

Project managed by Jessica Hodge
Designed by Andrew Barron
Printed in China

10 9 8 7 6 5 4 3 2 1

Every effort has been made to acknowledge
correct copyright of images where applicable.
Any errors or omissions are unintentional and
should be notified to the Publisher, who will
arrange for corrections to appear in any reprints.

FRONTISPIECE Moses, from the nineteenth-century
nave mosaics.
FRONT COVER The cloister walkway.
BACK COVER Detail of the reredos from
St Oswald's chapel.
FRONT COVER FLAP St Werburgh, from the
refectory window.
BACK COVER FLAP One of the saints portrayed in
the cloister glass.
INSIDE FRONT COVER FLAP Sixteenth-century ceiling
in the north transept.
INSIDE BACK COVER The cathedral seen across the
memorial garden.

All photography by Peter Smith unless
otherwise stated.

Mark Carline: pp. 7 far right, 18, 20 right, 30
Chester Cathedral: p. 71 above and below right
Angelo Hornak: pp. 2, 10 bottom left, 21 top
right, 25 far right, 26 left, 31 below right, 33
below right, 37, 41, 42 both, 54 right, 70 right, 72
Simon Warburton: p. 71 left